WILLIAM BUTLER,

Poems
2019 — 2023,

a collection of poems

ISBN: 978-969-41-9291-8

Graphics, design, and photography (except for author's portrait) by j roscoe phillips

me and the snow and the small grey cat

ovely powdery snow clinging to fence posts
car roofs and hoods
slickering the streets
so
I lace up the hiking boots
bundle in layers to brave the arctic blast
tip toe down the steps onto the drive
and
I am awkward biped
lurching to and fro
unbalanced but aware and alert
admire the wonderfully camouflaged landscape
but
a small grey cat sits watching
as I turn for home
as I almost fall
arms pinwheeling for foot purchase
it
daintily lifts one paw
(as if salute? in concert with me? in alarm?)
places that paw into the snow
stands and turns gracefully
shakes
that paw free of frozen water
steps politely to a fclinc rhythm
shaking each paw in turn
leisurely
retreats onto its porch free of snow
turns
and lifts a paw

On taking the last elevator up

How easy this is   should be
the hope in an extended   finger
thus

I've settled in now   the door closed
it is very warm   in here
going up

this man stares ahead   into his dream
we cannot   follow
Ding!

what would you say if I told you
this was the last elevator up?
there would be no others following

that man loves the   carpeting
admires it in   desperation?
appreciation?

and these women   these pretty women
laugh quietly   knowingly
hopefully

what would you say if I told you
this was your last up elevator?
we were the last ones in
alee alee Home Free!

Ding!
one last door sliding   open
each of us guessed correctly
each of us guessed wrong

it was never a guess

how it begins

we were candles in the quiet night
flickering for all others
steady for us
watching each other
eyes alert and on fire
her lips smiling
her face blushed in candlelight
and
in that instance
brief and strobe-like
each of us caught in lightning
fell
over and over and over
until we were caught
slowly
and breathlessly
together

Daytime Drinking

the uneven pavement from North Rampart to Frenchmen Street
to
Royal in the Quarter and into the cool chill of the Monteleon
Hotel breaks hearts
but
daytime drinking in New Orleans demands discipline and
courage
and
often that trek, quixotic as it may seem, reveals pure serendipity

Thursday is a mid day in my week
gathering energy for the coming
Friday through Sunday into itself
while poets and wanderers seek enlightenment in a cocktail
so to some cosmic confluence
some mystic casting of bones
two hoary such fellows
find refuge and solace
muted ages and wordsmithing
only by the absolving grace of daytime drinking

Sunday with the Brown Anole's

sunny mornings are quite regular here but today is moderate
in temperature with a frail breeze shimmying the green lace
tree in the backyard next door

I can stand on the steps behind my gate and stretch toward
the cloudless sky, my shadow disturbing the Brown Anole's
populating the city

I've disturbed their mating ritual for which they've prepared
these long months, and they are wary of any movement I
make as I sit to carefully observe
moments pass but finally they begin to move again, throat
pouches orange and pulsing as they move into and out of
the weeds next door

I speak softly to them explaining how they fit into this gar-
gantuan world for which they seem so ill-prepared. yet in
retrospect I think it is we who intrude

we who are newly raised up care nothing for the small
Brown Anole, the bee, the red and black flying bug annoying
my ankles as I sit and listen

we swat and complain and spray and curse those things
around us as if we are the species that can know, we can
only feel, and all else is slave

these moments make me uncomfortable, make me want to
step back inside my apartment and hide from the chastising
world busy in the daylight

now I have quite an audience of insects and Anole's hesitat-
ing at my fence secure in their status, in their seeming immu-
tability, while I can only watch

I hear them breathing

drowning man

she hesitated to turn the card to show him while staring
intently at it in her hand and the others standing uncomfort-
ably about him

some with broadening smiles more akin to sneers
but turning it she did, finally, her head down but kept her
hand on its upturned edge obscuring most of the card from
view then she laid it flat and pulled her jeweled hand away
his group had no idea what they were seeing other than
some semi-hocus pocus tarot fortune teller scamming their
friend out of $15 and at his insistence, too

he stared at the card
they stared at the card
so, he asked, cutting his eyes from left to right towards his
friends so they would know that he wasn't taking this seri-
ously, it was only a lark while they ambled about from bar to
bar
so, he asked more boldly, and the tarot reader who refused to
look up at him, spoke in a clear voice, you are the drowning
man, and this will be your fate from now until then
he was impatient, and in a rude and loud voice asked, what
am I drowning of and what do you mean from now until
then, that's not a time measurement that I know of
you are drowning in your self, you have become just you
and will only be just you with no room for anyone else to
breath with you, and you will be just you from now until
there is no more now

and if I grow too old to dream

I'll still have each memory
fading like old photographs
to leaf through
linger over
sipping my cooling coffee
at this desk
my morning bed in disarray
waits for my hands
forlornly welcomes me nightly
reminds me of its emptiness
and I conjure that memory
like an odd imprint on the sheets
cold dawns run together now
while I am warmed by night dreams
blending with todays distant sun
a wet paper watercolor
memorable and familiar and I dream on

the thin last light of day

how can you not love the thin last light of day
it dies to be reborn each dawn
fires the silent city
before life intrudes
quietens the rolling water
our boat ablaze in its flames
paints your face in soft colors
only I can see
smears the cobblestone streets
in dripping pastels
reminds us of the night
and softens its coming
reflects our days end
and promises tomorrow

man in red jacket falls

this is a quiet street, a dead end, culminating in a small
thicket of privet and deadfall cut by an active railroad track
people walk this street at times in errands both leisurely and
in haste

a group home is on this street with apartments inside and a
garage carved into several more

if I am passing my front windows my attention is piqued
now and then by someone walking by
a man in a red jacket falls but his two friends rush back to
help him up, brush him off, gather his things, walk on
the trio have bundles they carry
one has a Bug Bunny pack on his back, and a wad of clothes
tied with a belt

the weather is warming and soon I will sit on the side porch
and watch the street, and I will speak to those who walk by

I would know their stories but I draw back not wishing to
become part of their routine
we live in this world whether we recognize that or not, and
that street is your street, mine, these people our people
still I sit inside now and write about people I don't know,
stories I have not heard

the mystery in all of this, the unyielding truths we fear but
cannot confront is that we are afraid
our fears attach to various things - heights, people, the
future, the past, flying, insects, snakes, germs
our fears await us behind the doorway, down a dark
corridor, an echoing tunnel, they are real
a man in a red jacket falls,
and his companions rush to aid him

the light shining so bright

mid February and
blinded after indulging in that hot light all afternoon
but then as usual
smacked with the shocking cold water of real life
I
found myself absorbed in the unseen mating calls of hawks
raucous and urgent necessity
hidden in a tall jack pine
whose needles whistled in voyeuristic appreciation
magically heard and unseen
I
wanted to fly with them
an uncanny eye cast earthward
scanning for
for
what
my necessity
only to be blinded again
by the light shining so bright

low freight passing

echoing along the track
ice deadening this night stillness
and I wish
how i wish
I stood on my boat's bow
curl of foresail
curve of water breaking
each moment passing astern
and softening sunrise colors
peeking through the slot
but low freight train moans
no one to hear but me
and like catspaw wind shifts
it rolls away
and dreams shiver
fall crack
like ice from the ghost wires

vacation on Saturn

this is awesome!
it's not as forbidding as we were told
watching the rings
changing colors
the kaleidoscope wheeling through the black
but it is cold
bone-deep cold no matter what you wear
or the time of day or season
I can't say I wish you were here
or I will not say it
standing quietly in the lee of our AirBnB
an eternal whispering comes through
deepest darkest black space
the sensation of falling off is real
enhanced
the others are in the hot tub building
I can't hear them out here
how could we have not come here before?
how wonderful and awe-inspiring
my phone camera will not do it justice
I wonder where we will go next year?

song of the greyhound

its tires lulling us to sleep with some rubber mimicry of music
we nod and slide from side to side
dawn to midnight we slouch toward our fates
the greyhound delivers us
sings away hissing and spinning
where it was in the night air retains its image
each minor stop now rewarded
antiseptic-smelling waiting rooms
odd men eye-follow us
yesterdays coffee
our 'hound is home
above earth air water fire
it couples all together in some melding bond
sing onward
further
our greyhound
shining in early sun like a bullet
piercing fog banks and dawn deliveries
sudden counterpoint on a green-ensconced curve
shatters our awakening
we rise Venus-like
cheap overcoats our shell
each pair of eyes slide and slide again
the 'hound sings on
then we are there
an overture ends
brief coughing and rustling as we move about
and a last backward glance at our chariot
chuffing away in huffing diesel smoke
its song dims
disappears

when I dance

I dance alone to music I hear
no one to kibitz
no one to follow my leaden lead
no Astaire and no Kelly either
more Buster Keaton
but that adds a quaint fillip
imagining I dance on the ceiling
up the walls silently
so as not to alarm the neighbor
welcoming spring with Stravinsky
interpreting Dylan
flinging myself on the floor as Brown
my heart races and embraces the music
while I insure the blinds are drawn
and I dance with her who is not here
or in a vast line of dancers
here in the creaking wooden floored home
where I am safe
when I dance no matter the time
my head spins in rap rhythms
my feet follow

gnomes in the window

Ms Alma would have been a perfect grandmother
white haired and aproned
an aquarium and a window garden
peopled with gnomes
we
made butter we churned
we
learned to spool knit doilies
we
learned to hide from the radiation
under our heavy wooden desks
while
the gnomes watched
dark-eyed

the arc of the curve of the rainbow

it was there at once then fading   fading   faded
beheld in such awe and mystery
thrilling us at each turn in the road
fading   fading   faded
and then gone
neither the rainbow in its arc
its sweet curve toward the unreachable sky
then its collapse back to this solitary planet
nor our less admirable piecings
make any notice among the stars
what we believe from whatever source
is of no consequence
as the universe rages silently over us
and we are left alone
to remember only the arc of the curve of that last rainbow

when the party is over

this party is over
gather the pages, reams of written words
tidy up the place
tuck those good times away
scrapbook the photographs
push the bad memories under the bed
turn the book over
write on the cover
2022 Another Year
when the party is over
shut the door and close the blinds
stack the dishes in the sink for another day
linger over a shadow sitting on the kitchen stool
maybe a brief hint of perfume
try and remember what was said
who told you what
what promises you kept
those that fell away
this party is over
what was lost
what was gained
did you take two steps forward
three steps back?
did that sliver of hope cloud over?
winter sweeps under the baseboards
along the window sills
the old year takes a few final breaths
its eyes closed to the new
as ours are also
you cling to comfort and security
afraid now of what you don't know
what's to come
but like the passing year
it will be gone, too
that warm room

that already unraveling plan
this party's over
we had our say over cocktails
rending our clothes privately
scarring ourselves in the dark of the season
each day arrives slowly, tiredly
as old as the year past
limping along on worn legs
the party is over here
maybe has been for some time
we just turned out the lights
ignored the mess we made
preferring sleep
to reality's shine
and it's really all fine
reading (and writing) between the lines
waiting on the turntables needle to lift
find nothing else to translate
the party's over

a few back pages

wonder dreams are pieces of childhood fantasies
a puzzle we never completed now so much easier
trail through the woods whispering to us
marvels around each corner, each backyard
now they are brilliantly colored and vividly scored
as if we finally learned patience and listening
and my wonder at it all, these moments so personal
I press them tightly to my chest as if to imprint them

the impatience with tomato plants

I've had it growing those things I love so much
like so many things we sort through in life
the scrawny green stalk with two, three leaves
the oversize hole dug and a secret placed in it
watered, tended, nurtured during the eternity of spring
into the lull of summer it is my daily burden
the mystery unfolds one day as a green dot appears
 and another, more every day
each a reflection of our life, the dirt
powered by the sun and water
impatiently guarding the leafy stalk now
jealous of each passing night
black and green caterpillars with horns
chew the plant down to nubs
remind me of my fingernails
when as a child I nervously reduced them
and when the skeletal remains gently wave
one September morning
I rub the fragrant thickness of green
release the possibility of tomato
and make the exact vow each year
my impatience smoldering all winter long

small lessons

we live most of us remotely aware of what surrounds us
cracked cement and buckled asphalt fortify each street
crenellated fencing protecting the houses
while under the trees and weeds, the flowering plantings
truth teems eternally enshelled caparisoned
busy dealing with hunger and procreation
tragedy and hurried activity
some common goal reached endlessly
someone whispered to me
there is poetry under the stones
that pile of river rocks seethes with it
feverishly breaths life and truth
reveals the length and breadth of words
cycling through our attenuated lives
worn smooth in torrents here
these rocks left by glacial advance
shout and shale
demanding further recognition
all the while
a steam shovel scoops and deposits poetry
the leaf pile
rustles into truth
while we shop for groceries
deaf and blind
to our own end

the song of the one-armed gondolier

I do not sweep into the Grand Canal
I sweep the side canals of Zattare
in these tight side streets I am at my best
I sweep slowly and strongly with no rest
my right arm is twice as large as normal
I use my feet against the walls in traffic
I'll sweep you into the barcari for daily cicchetti
vino and glory of our water world
we will pass Cannaregio where I live
I have never been to the Lido
I have never seen Murano or Burano
I do not believe I've missed anything
but you will learn to love Venezia as we do
see! you can watch fish now swimming along
when you sweep with the one-armed gondolier
who sits waiting on tide and you

Dermis

I am looking,
searching
under my eye lids
mine as heavy as my mothers
creased folds;
early morning
darkness.
I can see through
my shut eyes,
see beyond the shadow brother,
see through the veil
as it lifts;
bright unexpected light blinds me.
I hold my hand before
my face in the dark,
see the skin
that first layer
revealing the dermis,
then
looking closely,
my hand against my eyes,
I see the tiny vessels
Ceaselessly
pulsing.
I am afraid
in the dark that all will stop.

reliquary

it is a simple, small wooden box I've kept about since the 70's
periodically I open it and touch various things contained
touch them to establish their reality as part of my reality
some have meaning and history easily discerned
some have iconic value

and a scant few have only vague memory attached
trailing like wisps of cloud
there are paperclips and clasps
recent objects still fragrant with their memory
mundane pieces, too

as well as one or two savagely spiritual objects
here a medal from some foot race

underneath that sea glass from an island
an insignia for a uniform

a tattered piece of green ribbon from a gift
an errant earring, just one

the box is packed
and never locked but I resist opening it often
for fear the memories will
like Pandoras mistake

scatter about and be lost
it is my scrapbook of old yellowing photographs
more vividly recalling moments than any album
so I sit and mutter over them
aging apotropaist

in his magic domain

rock boy stream

water noise feet on rock beach
he leans over easily
fetching rock hurling it into stream
the shape of water accepting it
that noise
he and his friends his brother
all tossing rocks into the happy stream
laughter and shouts
memories
each in turn and together
I feel the flood in my heart
carried along back to then
away from now
rock boy stream

One Small Leaf

On a day much like this one day,
on the trails meandering along the muddy course
of this narrow river,
after rain, chilly,
my feet wet but that unfelt,
I leaned against a tree momentarily,
freed my shoes of clinging mud,
and felt the tickle,
the trickle of one small leaf
as it fell and rested against my neck
like a cold snail,
foreign but not unwelcome.
I reached for it,
felt the coming of its brittleness,
the rows of veins,
how simply spaced, how sensibly perfect.
I knew it from late winters budding,
springs encouragement, summers wilt,
and every night it had stirred,
communed with other leaves.
It was jewel-like in perfection,
yet softly curling against my coarse fingers.
As all things, it was returning to its origins.
Accepting and rejoicing in mute simplicity.
I turned and went on my way,
a mild jog and back,
but as I passed that same tree,
several more leaves fell,
and I begin to see how the path opens for us,
endless in its awareness,
its truth.
Paths like this
filled with light and love
carry us forever

a pair of shoes

our thrift store meander starts sullenly
        among the housewares
leaning toward each other
telling
            stories of a lifetime length
cracked platters and tarnished silverware

wearables askew on hangars
    each smells of its former owner
buttons missing
        zipper
    rusted   swollen along the seams

mama has an umbrella in bright red
wooden handle beauty
        warding off the sun or rain in turn

but the kid   stooped over in the aisle
            struggling
not his size   not yet his size
Michael Jordan logo basketball shoes
    or for his beats career
boasting in the school corridor how he found them
    those   shoes
his smile mimicking the Nike logo
broad   thick   eternal
    a pair of shoes

night hurries down

those days when all else sharply focused on the most trivial of
moments
hurried coffee and unappetizing lunch
quickly forgotten
when five o'clock retreated up the clock face
the work day was twelve hours long
all that pushed aside in the rush to be elsewhere
then elsewhere surrounded by promises and unfiltered dreams
Miles on the turntable
gin bottle on the kitchen counter
ice cold vermouth and an olive
semi-dark lit only by candles
headlights on the window
bed turned down anticipating lovers
smiling in the candleshadow lovestruck
giddy laughter and eyes shining like a mirrorball
moving bodies as if dancing
she laughs when the bed complains
we watch each other softly
night hurries down

just float

my hand against the current
trilling creek water over rocks
colors vibrate
just float
relax
flow
sails shadow my silhouette
water over the bow flashes
my face blank
just float
noiseless
mute
what else is there to see save sky and cloud
just float
what troubles are there but eddies and pools
just float
this wave lifts me from reverie
this one spins me like a top
this one is translucent
this one speaks loudly
just float

a red ball

it is a stormy day
clouds threatening the tree tops
"splots" of fat rain drops pop my hat
down my neighbors driveway
a bright red ball
slowly rolls
my hands reach for it
I bend at the waist
how green the pines
nodding to the winds
rain smell brings memories

mending

her arthritically knotted fingers hovering
over the tiny flaws
I'd rent in my sweater
never ceased until the cloth was whole
and made wearable again
presentable for elementary school
I imagined her repairing my soul, too
its flaws widening
glaringly evident to all
who passed me by in my anonymity
while those gentle hands
and supple fingers
flew among the tears and holes
precisely and quickly
before those flaws
could claim me

Toy Aisle at WalMart

I only wanted to look at the action figures
a hint into the soul of a six year old
birthdays and Christmas to come
overwhelmed by the sheer variety
shelves bulging with color and noise
little kid wandered up
his eyes truly glowing with anticipation
tugged at my shirt sleeve
fixated as he was on a Batman motorcycle box
slowly turned his head first
then his eyes up to me
finding no father or mother
but me
and fled
an aisle over her voice scolding
I guessed the mother
I told you not to wander around, didn't I?
now you just keep your hand on the cart
stay right where I can see you
somebody gonna steal you away!
a child's dreams and fears
worlds colliding, crumbling
over a Batman motorcycle toy
gleaming in its box
"Try Me!" button in bold colors
guarded by some old guy
his mother couldn't trust
couldn't even see
in that moment
I would've bought the toy aisle
presented it to each kid
the aisle in all its out-of-reach glory
for a gentle tug on my shirt sleeve

what I carry in my possibles

it is a small bag, rough looking, and depthless
with my possibles all arranged
at least whenI first packed;
there are my promises, odd-sized different ages, some on
paper folded countless times, some newly folded;
pictures of my sons, their families, and my mom and dad,
sister,
group picture of grandkids;
a book of dreams and one of hopes, that one in shreds,
and a thick book of my past, a thinner one of my future.
Some necessaries, some frivolous toys - harmonica, spinning
top, magnets, a kids kaleidoscope, deck of cards (but only 48
in the deck),and a book, thick with stories by various au-
thors, change of jeans, blue silk bandana, sweat band.
That's about it.
My hats I keep always ready to travel; so essential to me
they aren't possibles but necessities.
In the deepest, darkest depth I keep a photo of you, and I
pull it out now and then, turn it over several times, run my
fingers over it, and put it away.
All things in my possibles.
some have meaning and history easily discerned
some have iconic value
and a scant few have only vague memory attached
trailing like wisps of cloud
there are paperclips and clasps
recent objects still fragrant with their memory
mundane pieces, too
as well as one or two savagely spiritual objects
here a medal from some foot race
underneath that sea glass from an island
an insignia for a uniform
a tattered piece of green ribbon from a gift
an errant earring, just one
the box is packed

and never locked but I resist opening it often
for fear the memories will
like Pandoras mistake
scatter about and be lost
it is my scrapbook of old yellowing photographs
more vividly recalling moments than any album
so I sit and mutter over them
aging apotropaist
in his magic domain

provinces of the heart

we created the hallowed provinces
that only the heart can define
tended them with careful hands
shaped and molded them in some fashion
not all of our making or design
those secret places
those sacred places
known only to each
lest we forget a province
lest we forget the care, the passion
our eye may momentarily move away
within the vivid boundaries of a province
lighted like the new universe
dance the music we have made
we tend those provinces that shape us
until the last moment of light
and we fade into obscurity
relishing those new provinces
revealed as we flash

winds leaves freight trains

the freight train blues brokenly
skyscape grey and cold
my deadend street solemn

only the skittering wind moves
privet shields the train from us
I hear echoes from the tracks

pecan tree leaves hustle and bunch
seemingly finding comfort
creatively tossing into piles

there is a hollowness along here
deadening sound and color
our monotone moments alone

but I can hear her clearly now
whispering whatever I wish of her
and my ears burn with our secrets

this is my garden

I have heard the words I wrote
I've read them again
and yet again
and I have given them to you
to do with as you may
while I in my garden
am sitting against an old wooden fence
split and worn grey as my hair
listening to the woodpecker
the dove cooing
squirrels fussing

I see clouds scudding by
hurrying away
while I wait to hear words come sing to me

what you will do with my words
I do not know
nor do I know the purpose of this
but to offer their singing to you

I step in the path of my forest among the tombstone trees
in no hurry
and I watch things move and appear
magically about their business
whether I tarry or not

this piece of world is mine while I am on it
my ownership as momentary as a breath
a sharp inhalation
a step
the singing is for me
I will remember the words
I will remember the songs

but now they are yours

me and possum

after the rain, the lightning, the thunder
my tight passageway walk is mossed over
bright green against the age-blackened brick
rivulets gurgling toward the gate and street
like so many rains I've enjoyed in my life
temperatures reduced,
streets steaming
and old possum
living in the abandoned house next door
hunkers atop the wooden fence
his intent at camouflage negligible
he hisses, resolved not to play dead
          so I step back, giving him free way
but I don't retreat
          he rises, nods, begins that odd walk
          keeping me within his side eye
reaches the wire, climbs down, awkwardly,
          into the wet and leaning weeds
me and old possum
if not friends
at least nodding acquaintances

blind man on Frenchman Street

tap tap tap
slowly making his blind way
broken pavement
misaligned bricks and chipped cobbles
Sunday morning Frenchman Street
he steps over brown glass
his cane sweeps past plastic cups
tap tap tap
halts at Decatur
stands head cocked listening
bars closed this early morning
music venues doors closed and locked
his white shirt fresh and starched
tap tap tatatap
finds the curb at Chartres
pauses attentively
steps down
tap tap tap to Royal
crossing the street there
feels the shadow of Washington Square Park
the shade deep this morning
taptaptaptap
along the metal fencing

he sits now with his cane between his legs
listening to barking dogs
voices around him
isolated in his lost sight

a passerby in sprung top hat passes
pauses
speaks
are you having a good morning walk?
he says with no trace of amusement
it's just been beautiful

and so it is

fulgurites

my John the conqueroo
my Third Eye Hand
a painted and sequined fava bean
yak bone mandala
1/6 domino I carry in my watch pocket

lode stones and lucky charms
I speak quietly and reverently to black cats
never look over my left shoulder
I keep two pennies with me
I wear two different socks

I switch my watch from wrist to wrist
stand on one leg
stretch to the sun salute
to the dog
to my aching vertebrae

I cannot watch the zapruder film
tragedy hewn from our tears and isolations
one story regales
one story is askew
one is awry

music threads my tears and rents
patches my lonely heart
words bind themselves to the music
visions are in technicolor
butlers have closets named after them

we have always been here
look in our outstretched hands
an owl feather a river stone a sea shell a bead bird from
Mexico
window stickers
my scars and injuries

we bought from two brothers on Belvedere
swam in the fountain
trippy and mad
and I read Cavafy to them
cheering each ripple

we drank and ate and swam in our minds
colors and tide charts irrelevant
only the soft swarm of metaphor
against the placid island
we found in our dreams

and later in Honduras
then in Belize
under the tube of light
a universe into itself
bloomed and beckoned

butterfly garden

the butterfly garden is quiet today in
autumns threatening night

chill, and the empty mesh cages where
we held out our hands for

them to flutter indecisively forward
then settle on our fingers like

so many exotic jeweled rings,
hold only us, standing monstrously,

speechless, and aware of how awkward
and dull we are

clothesline

smell the sunshine clothes on the line
reminders
drift through the flapping
breeze picked up
green lace tree shaking like Chris Owens
reminders

empty clothesline whipping in the rain
sings of family secrets revealed
reminders
rain drops big as plates
runnels gurgling toward the river
reminders

oleander blossoms welcome my step
dusty palmetto stiffens
reminders
sheds rain in a frenzied curve
all confusion washed away
reminders

b yo fool

he said b yo fool to no one in particular as I was walking by
him leaning into his hands resting on his knees seated on a
green metal and wooden bench along Decatur Street

I thought about going back and asking him to clarify what
he had been a fool about seated there his wool knit cap
askew in today's swirling winds scattering

tourists and plastic bags and tall skinny daiquiri cups
around the streets of the Vieux Carre thought about it only
but didn't actually turn around

just kept walking toward Canal Street my mood elevated by
someone's pithy and mysterious remark fueled by whatever
had been in the empty

bottle rolling around under his bench and I noted then how
scurrying everyone seemed to be in an immediate errand it
seemed

while I merely wanted the exercise the moments alone walk-
ing gathering threads of wisdom and ideas and resolutions
and chucking them

all under the trolley once I was on Canal Street its stridently
clanging bell summoning such detritus jarringly so I turned
there

found my way to Rampart and bruised by that fierce north
wind cast my eyes toward home

watching the street

to see if the grey car drives up, turns into my driveway
I know beforehand it is momentary
what isn't
but I also know to preserve these moments
(for truly that is what they are)
in perpetuity there in my frontal lobe
her smile and obvious joy
being here
those seconds
painted in vivid
(not somber)
colors on the walls of my heart
all while watching the street

x-ray

dark was made light again
over the small coffee

in the small coffee shop
over small talk

and memories packed away
almost forgotten until

reminded by the hands
holding the small coffee cup

becoming lovers sooner
than imagined

after x-rays revealed
starving hearts

and the bones in
the lovely hands

were empty

topography of the heart

the heart is a quiet desert
until love seduces it

lush dense foliage results
flowering vines and jasmine hedges

lovers words and slow hands
bring it to full bloom

the city sings its dreams

wake now with the pity and the drying bones
the city sings its dreams
we hear the melody but do not understand the lyrics
echoes in the square color street lights
smear the song in lavish concrete
inculcated into the chorus

why can't we hear that singing
our city turning away
no longer a simple carousel tune

the city turning on its dime
forgets clapping hands
and dancers in the round
no longer a piece of it all
a mere chord progression
and the rivers sweet harmonica

rough chapped

his hands were huge and chapped and
rough as sandpaper, reddened from the cold
and immersion in icy water checking
his 75 Lb fishing line
tediously tied to the plastic milk jugs
floating on the lively White River that icy
morning

the aluminum Jon boat an icebox
metal thwarts like sitting on knives
he had no other trade nor means
and his trailer on a bare patch of woods
dangling with forgotten
insulation just off the gravel
road leading deep into
a state forest bore a thin
metal chimney cut into the roof
serving a wood stove

winter meant hard he said harder
than any other season and it
toughened him for the following months
when spring rain and tornadoes swept
patches of forest like so much stubble
across the forgotten and fallow fields

but he was there and meant to stay there
until something or someone drove
him away
like an ancient tree whose roots
tap unseen
into the darker heart of the earth
he said
I got nothin else

differences

when morning seeps under my winter window blinds
and cold nights monsters quieten
I offer a prayer to the Siddhartha Gautama
serenely perched on my chest of drawers
strike another day from my calendar
gather my past into a neat pile
pause over its immensity
weighing
the differences
between then and the Now
bow again to them all and salute the moment

I will live in this day
before it's discarded this night
adding its collective sighs celebrations sadness and
realizations quietly again
I will See each minute and each face surrounding me
in that moment clearly
offering neither pro nor con
but smiling into my sleeve
at the starred universe of it All

it only took a second and I was washed in the blood of the lamb

every small gesture rewards in its way
every kindness offered to another, too

and that opportunity presents itself
daily on my walks here in this community

where the grifter and the con
the junkie and the runaway

strum guitars and water their dogs
under balconies and in hedges

but she seemed terribly old
seated in her wheelchair

the wheels planted in a French Quarter hole
teetering on the brink of the broken asphalt

and I in the moment
offered

bumping the chair and woman
onto the smoother sidewalk

 chair and woman of negligible weight
like some ephemeral gossamer fabric

and was blessed in muffled tones
offered His Blood

washed as it were
in the Blood of the Lamb

the lonesome lizard king of bywater

squatting in the chill February wind by the side of the
colorful creole cottage, the lonesome lizard king of bywater

hears an echo, his head turning to the side better to see the
neighborhood, check for traffic on the pitted streets

stumbling residents coming back from a parade laughing
and holding one anothers arms for support

tourists with backpacks and cell phone cameras tilted up or
over, eager to catch a memory of the place

and the echo fades, just another faint hope his lady fair
lizard queen would tear herself away

from whatever held her from him, her voice now only an
echo so long she has been gone

but he rises to his full height, his throat pouch filling and he
gives vent to his frustration, his loss

still the lonely lizard king of bywater and still pining for his
queen and the warmth of spring sun

dreams like pecan pralines on a hot day

her delicate hands delivered them to me wrapped in flimsy paper
     my hands sweating already from the brief walk
I am apprehensive
               it is in a dream
     I can smell them right now and I always will smell them
no matter   where I am
     she smiles sweetly sugary melting any misgivings
feigns interest in my babbling   takes payment
          two small coins   one for each eye
               as is the custom for the dead
                    paying tariff
do I walk out of the door?
                    does she merely fade away?
while my hands   sweet and sugary now   beckon
          my dreams are not yours not anymore
but
               cannot you smell those pralines
                    that caramel-like sugar
it is as real as you   or as me   or anyone reading this
               so learn to always carry
                    two small coins
                    for the tariff

I find you

I find you while walking around the house
opening the chest of drawers
there those hand-made pajama bottoms

I wear in the coldest months of the year
and an emerald sleep set
I bought for you and you

wore once or twice to please me
rest in solemn wait while in the closet a hat I bought
when we strolled along the giddy streets

holding hands like teenage lovers
our ears alert to each other
eyes smiling into the cool night air

I find you

and now it's too late

holding out your arm so we can check the time again
but we already knew and now it's too late
to hold back the faint tide

where we walked and talked yesterday
answering the questions we answered before
disappeared in that unnoticed pull

the moon coldly evaluating our hearts
weighing us solemnly and silently
then passing on

and now it's too late to evaluate
our eyes closed, mouths open
vain hope we will capture the moment

we are like strangers in a dark tunnel
afraid to touch, to ask
fearful of our knowing

I had flowers for you

and along the way that long circuitous way
my flowers for you shed
and when I arrived at your door so late so
long after late for you
looking back along my way as
far as I could see were the petals
of your flowers I forgot to give to you
so long ago and so many miles
away but here
I am now with my crooked smile
matching the crooked miles I walked
carrying your flowers
that left their petals
to mark our way back

November rain

gently
early November morning rain summons the old king

he shuffles slowly along
emptied and fulfilled in his term

we turn our heads away
not in deference but pity at his infirmities

now come the weeks of anticipation
for the new king brought from the old

a ritual accompanied by body-felt hymns
the elder oaks nod and sway, bowing to his coming

while we in our own elder years
stand mutely swaying to the elemental rhythms

voicing under our breaths the ancient words
the king is dead long live the king

anticipating we will endure spring and summer
with no sense of autumn or winter

holding those distant and vague times
as if in our dreams

falling into oleander

my nose wrinkles at wisteria
that scent familiar, recognizable
its vines sag under the weight
its blooming brief and sudden
while today my left toes
casually following the right's
tossed me loosely into oleander
the bush huge and luxurious
pink blossoms showering me
and the mule-drawn tour carriage
clopping steadily beside me
had a comic moment to share
while I leaning into the tall shrub
suffered neither concern
or embarrassment
only intoxication
older Ulysses enticed
again by the lotus fruit

impermanence

I taste the fat flakes with my curling tongue stuck out
eyelids wetted
then we walked to school kicking snow at girls
each other

during basic training it snowed as we marched
hand to hand combat a farce
the slick sided pit frozen and slushy and we were thirsty
I stuck my tongue out as we marched back

each snowfall meets incredulity
how could it be
how much will it be
snow-angel prints appear
red-faced kids

I walk to the coffee house bundled but with my tongue out
a snowman greets me down the block
huge green and brown ears
remnants of a banana tree

are the streets icy
when will it melt
cabin fever
wood burning in the fireplace

all of this now
then forgotten as crocuses poke heads up
buds on tulip poplar trees appear

I stick my tongue out
spring has a taste
like new-plowed earth
fresh turnings

I wanted to write a love song

I wanted to write a love song, sing it
quietly to you after you were asleep
one night,

feel your heart slow and in nights
rhythm, your breathing, I
whisper to

you how I, like a child, skip through the
day remembering that the light
loves you

and how quickly each clock's turnings
bring us each other in measures only
we will ever know.

fugue in blue
part 1

what cannot be held but holds
someone asked

starting from my chair I cannot see
but I can determine

clarity isn't a particular state
it is a certainty

her back to me wrapped in green
isn't a final gesture

my morning coffee presents the day
while I salute the former night

if I can't remember the lessons
will you let me peek

blues burn hot at midnight
scorched the wooden floor

memory is an exercise
a deep bend and squat

this is only part of the lesson
you must hold onto it

peintures

stepping across wet cardboard I slip
rain-slicked sidewalk

his fingers comb the lank hair from his face
he says, excuse my mess

his rain-wet jeans and soggy shoes smell
he leans against the painted wall

plastic flagging from the street repairs
cover his possessions

next to him are paintings
on wet brown cardboard

a cat a dog shadowed street lights
and an angel hovering

while he holds at bay the restless world
under my feet we spin

gimme wachu got

what he said
standing outside Kroger
an older woman fumbling in her worn purse
digging as deeply as if for a core sample
a taste of what lies beneath the mantle
her run over shoes
cotton coat on this blustery day
cracked lens eyeglasses

but she dug and dug
at last came up with a bill
maybe a single
maybe a five
offering it in supplicant hands
to that young man
in flame printed hoodie
cap askew
brilliant white sneakers

what did he say to her offering
what did she say over the offering

we hurry past to and from our cars
pushing clanking wobbling grocery carts
unloading our guilt
balanced on our feet
hurrying
downward glancing
up at waiting vehicles

did she know him
her suitor
her son
her nephew
demanding tribute
and where were we
avoiding this struggle
no not anything to do with me
I didn't see anything
he said what

it has come to this

watching a woman on NOLA's riverwalk

she walks along the rivers edge
her pockets filled with memories

keeps one hand free
and the other filled with regrets

now and again she switches hands
tells us she will never forget

each moment behind her
while the coming moments strands

find room in the empty pocket
a final resting place for their weltschmerz

stuck inside of memphis with those NOLA blues again

ain't nobody care
swat he said to me
waitin in the ER like a fool
bleedin on he shoes
she just bought em for him too
like holden his head with one hand
swattin em chirruns wif the other
n ain't nobody
I mean Nobody care

words tumbling like two cup dice
spill out on the world
while I'm in the grocery checkout line

I wanna know more
my five day stubble free entry
while my face shines like a flashlight

where do I fit I wanna ask
but would anyone there know
or care one tiny bit

and the colors and the hours swirl
until I'm back on Elysian Fields
working women hurrying to buy lunch
kid in tow
get'em to school

we talk there
maybe even laugh at this monumental joke
this shared vibe together

gold teeth flash and braid extensions slash
spandex and yoga pants
my straw hat and ink instant admission

but reality is a sawdust sandwich
I choke down without a daiquiri
turn and find the line moved on

the day it started to rain

it was the day it started to rain then thought better of it
made the clouds sull up, spit shut
sun struck the band on Royal at Frenchmen Street
kepi hats white shirts black ties black trousers
the bass drummer sitting down to play
and I stood
sweat pouring down my eager white face
looking up that street
lost in a fantasy so sweet it made speech
a foreign tongue

my shoes turned the corner slapping a rhythm for me
and the bakery
its doors open to us all
whispered what our treat would be
when the day it started to rain
breaks open again

monsoon

listening as I sit with my cafe au lait
almond croissant
civilized at 9:30
in the Big Easy
listening in a way
one ear while sorting through my history
mine
until I hear
and she spiked his drink, burned his clothes in her fireplace
December, just before Christmas
and
then I am listening
she went on
tied him to her bed, a four poster
by then I needed descriptions
butt naked
hired two very large naked women to get in bed with him
when he woke up
veined white's of his eyes, hair tousled,
stupid open mouth
that's what I am hearing
she takes several photographs
tosses him a red terrycloth robe
see what I mean, descriptions
had the "models" dress and leave
cuts his plastic tie from his left hand
tosses a box cutter on the bed and leaves him there
she mailed the pictures to his wife

then these two women are done
stand and leave

there is the karmic cloud descending on that scene
and I can walk on shaking my head
staring at the uneven sidewalk of Decatur

woman eating beignets in the French Market

powdered sugar flies lightly about her head
the simple black tee shirt dusted
telling her friend and the rest of us, too
she weighed almost 300 pounds eleven years ago
had a bypass
lost 175 pounds
one year at Jazz Fest
had to have three security guards pick her up
in the Louisiana tent
zydeco and cajun two step
she laughs
divorced now the sugar almost a mist
her chins wobble with each bite
sorry weight loss reduced her boobs
has excess flesh around her middle
best beignets in New Orleans
Loretta's Authentic Pralines
going to dance practice tomorrow
Sunday
practicing for Krewe of Boo parade
she seems fond of her dancing
the KamelToes
I burp po boy and soda
but
there it is
whatever you are do become wish to be fantasize about
New Orleans has a place for you
loves you when no other will

Her Fingers

Her fingers
catch in her hair,
an innocent enough gesture,
a thing she does, I do, we do,
and suddenly she is a younger girl,
young woman,
in her shorts and loose top
defying the Memphis June heat.
And I can only look,
hoping my mouth isn't agape,
and study her until I feel her discomfort,
and there!
she does that again.
I would catch her hair,
bring it to my face,
luxuriate in it,
her smell, fresh, soap, clean.
then carry her away from here,
from this mundane, this being here,
when I believe all she needs is me.
In my vanity.

She Lives in the Mirror

I lost her in the mirror behind that bar,
lost her as surely as if I'd walked out on her,
or her on me,
but tonight
she lives in the mirror behind that bar,
I know,
I saw her there,
still smiling, mischievous eyes,
lips full and slightly parted
as if she wanted to tell me a secret.
What? No, I'm ok, I told the bartender.
I just wanted to stare at her,
reach through that mirror,
touch her, listen to her.
I'm deaf but my heart hears.
I am blind but my heart can see.
Sure, another one for me,
rye, no ice, thanks.
How many is that now? Four.
I'm ok then. One more
then I'll have to leave her here to another man.
I'll walk back. Dark and cold.
She'll whisper secrets to that new guy.
Why not? She's a beautiful woman.
Maybe I'll find her tomorrow night,
and maybe I won't.
It's too late now to think about it.

I'm at the end of the bar

cloudy and sullen skies
June in New Orleans
oleander blossoms on my hat
Ryan's Irish Pub, Decatur at Bienville
$5 Irish Car Bombs daily
Happy Hour from opening to close
I'm at the end of the bar
cool and dark in there, quiet now
afternoon drinking just one pint o'Guiness
reflecting on divergent paths these feet have taken me
none straight and few narrow
struggles and endless hilarity
depressions and elations
loves and many, many losses
women and yes, even men I've loved, love
miss
hearing voices echoing today
what I wouldn't give......
naw, I've given too much as it is
what I am I accept now in some measure
always an eye open towards change
minor it may be
and always
always looking forward to another adventure
new people old friends happy faces
and those depth plumbing sad moments, too
like old wounds and fading scars
I'm at the end of the bar

**I'm at the end of the bar
(partie deux)**

and the music has faded away so now we listen to the
bartenders favorites
and the carnival closed its doors
tents are dark
the musicians packing up instruments
speak quietly to one another
good night good night
so the quiet I wish for is never there
voices compel me to the riverside
along the railing
safely
old crimes adjudicated
dark rolling this way upriver
thunder roils the faint outline of clouds
we scud home
ahead of the faint lights
smearing in mist and summer rain
until tomorrow
when we will be here agin

Moment

it was as if I were there again
	with you in the moment
sandy breeze from water to beach
night crawling forward with our shadows
		moon flashlight bright
tide washing footprints away behind us
no one could follow us then
		watching you move

all of this from one picture

what else is stored away within our hearts
what else can be recalled in these vivid colors

how else can I say we are like one person
thing
whether we are together
or
at whatever distance

writing a lifetime of passion, framed in our boundaries
	when we have only had moments
how grateful I am for those times I can fondly remember
my face blurring in the effort
	you bending to kiss me
me bending to you on the soft brown bed
forever caught in our moment

the gandy dancers waltz

it is early light along the tracks
    men gather at the cut
tools wait on the rail flat car
    tamping bars, claw bars, picks, lining bars
strange shapes mixed into the familiar

the men sort themselves into clots
    move ethereally in the morning mist
muffled metal noises follow them
    their reality begins
oversized pants and jackets against the chill

one man calls, Wake up Jacob!
    his railroad hat askew
men answer with a grunt and heave of steel
    Early in the morning!
Tamp er Down!

a length of steel rail dark in this light
    UnH!
their feet waltz-like move backward
    slide forward again
steel laid in ballast rock

Whachu gonna do for breakfast?
    Eat at steel, lay em Down!
step, slide, Unh! bend and grunt
    thin sun leaks into the cut
human steam rises with them

another clot dances into the cut
    long steel lining bars glint
Turn em Out!
    his voice echoes out of the cut
HunH! picks and shovels at work

they dance here for two days
   dawn until 5 with breaks at times
water on the rail flat car
   metal lunch pails at noon
then they are gone

they have faded now into that heavy morning mist
a last faint call is never answered again
the gandy dancers elegant waltz
only a memory

What She Means To Me

her eyes tell me to give more than I can take
tell her the truth
make it all real
in all ways, always
put a little sugar in her bowl
said she'd be there for me
rock my soul
those eyes holding mine
I'm lost
smiling at me
she takes my breath
leaves me tongue-tied at best
writing verse and rhymes
walking through town absent minded
her hand hot in mine
laughingly tells me she'll stay
one more night
to dance our way down dark streets
made suddenly light as day
whatever comes
we deal with in our way
words pour out like trinkets
I decorate the world in three quarter time
footsteps echoing as one
then we're home
and she's all mine.

walking

there is a story here in these trees in this old park
many stories carved in the trails and the old trees
and if you are still on a still day and listen
you will hear the overstory retelling the stories
bending to one another
as old men will do

walking on a sunny still day without the swirl of leaves
city noises distant and indefinable
slowly turn your head and watch the slight nod
the bowing of the old trees
as they watch you
aware of what we bring
and leave

within the overstory bare now of leaves and mist
rare and unseen bird life gives quiet evidence
learns how to live in the new nakedness
soft wings spread and they take flight
noiseless as the forest
suggesting to us mysteries
long unsolved

walking among the trees in this old park

those things we always remember

there is a rain tonight
and
there is a wind tonight
under the dome of night sky
those clouds we remember
flee towards the east north-east

do you ever look up in the sky
the night sky
and sigh with the passing of time

does the rain hear you
and
does the wind hear you

the night air smells of summer
and
you one gentle night when the wind
stirring wisteria and shiny oak leaves
opened to wonder

it is a night of rain
and
a night of wind
and this house creaks and pops
remembering others footsteps
others memories

like those things we always remember

this boy

he looked like a lonely boy
staring off into the flood
crowds surging past him
the walkway juddering
his arms shaking as he leaned on the metal railing

but his feet tapped in rhythm with the music
shirt tail flapping behind him
ignoring the hubbub
alone it seemed this boy
part of it all but not

some piece of me stood there, too
caught in the mystic
aware of the push and pull
river boiling past
every part of me in rhythm

and then I'm carried along
toward some distant place
where I must be part of it
part of the body like the river
floating away
away
and away

mean angels

look at'em sittin at the end of the dark bar tellin stories
cuttin their eyes at everybody else quiet like so nobody else
can hear'em
mean angels nursin a glass of beer or a half empty shot
payin no mind to anybody but aware of us all sittin at the
other end
they got some mean eyes, drunk's eyes but that don't mean a
thing cause you know angels can handle their selves
handle us, too, and countin the house
two old men with missin teeth
guy I guess got kicked out his house and he looks as mean as
they do 'cept he's by hissef empty stool both sides of him
biker dude in leathers and greasy hair
Sue from down the street been livin' in here dyin' in real
time got that crooked lipstick smeared on her teeth grinnin'

and then there's me

The loneliest Rooster in City Park

I like Sunday mornings at the public track in City Park, NOLA; it brings out a cast of characters including me who slog or walk or jog the 400m oval with its deep and over-grown infield and surrounding grounds. Parking spaces are plentiful and there are two porta-lets handy although wasps thrive in one and the City seems to ignore them regularly. The track is on the north end of the park near Lake Poncha-train, and the roadways that network through the graceful oak trees, the soccer and rugby fields, baseball diamonds, lakes, bayous, NOMA and its sculpture garden, the pedal boat lake, two golf courses, disc golf area, picnickers, stroll-ers, mother's with strollers, lovers, lurkers, and Cafe du Monde bring it all together.

The Park is 170 years old, 1300 acres, one of the United States largest urban parks catering to all sorts of pursuits. It presents three stadiums including one in which the Pan American Games were held back in the nineties. In fact there are two very old hurdles leaning forlornly in high grass on one straightway that so designate themselves as having been part of those games. They seem as old and tired as I will be soon enough on my last loop.

Today, this morning, as I looped another 400m on my quest for 6400m, a sudden crowing sounded in the copse of oaks bordering the oval, definitely a crowing which I ignored on that loop. On subsequent passes on that unforgiving, syn-thetic surfaced track, radiating heat up through the soles of my New Balance's and down through the crown of my sun hat, the crowing continued for some period. Finally I noticed another denizen of the Sunday track squad passing me and I hailed him down, "Is that a rooster,?" I inquired.
"No, that's a chicken," he replied. So there.

Finally my curiosity magnified the crowing and I strolled off the track and walked along the street until I was opposite the trees from which that crowing resounded. I slowly stalked into the copse, peering upwards, and as I crackled on another felled pile of sticks, the damn thing flew, yes, flew from just above my head to a neighboring tree whose lower limbs actually drape onto the ground. It was a garishly-colored fowl, definitely a rooster, and as I stood there a passing runner said, "rooster been there a while, heard'em every day I get up here." And to his fleeing back I said, "must be lonely with no hens," and never heard a reply or a guffaw nor did I see a slight turn of head.

And in reflection I must admit I felt some kinship with that solitary rooster. Here I was in an adopted city, walking a hot track among people who although friendly enough are not people I know or will ever know. I cannot crow, so I silently lament that sense of alone-ness that comes with being solitary, and I assure you it is voluntary. As often as not I presume someone I have a brief conversation with will recognize a like soul, and we will have some further relationship, but as with all us old roosters, once the crowing is done, we are content to sit and watch the parade pass having offered what we consider our finest offering, and can now ruminate about brief moments such as this.

what surprises still await

we who don't look
we who are slow to recognize
find surprises still wait
and so it was
innocently?
I believe
Yes
but therein lies the simplest surprise
her smile
her eyes betraying something more
her soft hand
and each morning
she would be
my surprise
after all else had failed

seeing

harsh morning when all seemed to
blur but one weird spot
completely blank in my right eye

trying to first remember what if
anything had happened
the night before to my eyes

then reflecting on the fragility of my
poor body in apparent
enthusiastic revolution

my mirror reflecting an innocent face
unshaven and mussed
from sleep while I canted my head

to and fro to catch whatever was
blinding me to the days events,
to the promise of a book unread, a face

unmemorized yet finding no solace
nothing to blame or repair
then waiting for a doctor's verdict

while he peered deeply into my soul
through my broken eyes
declaring a dead retina and fear of a

future of eventual blindness for
which I could make no plan
rendering my love for books and reading

a distant pleasure

she kept her fears under her bed

where she peeked at them each night before closing her eyes,
never once bringing them out into the open, perferring to
keep them secreted away from anyone else's eyes.

those of you who knew her, had known her for some time
were in awe of her fearlessness, her wit and humor, her fath-
omless intelligence, her unerring ability to listen.

she would remind us that we must face our fears if we wish
to understand and thus eliminate or subordinate them, even
quoting Jung on understanding fear.

after she became ill in her late years many of us had moved
away or lost contact with her but as she entered hospice, she
had the strength left to summon several of us.

her room in the hospice residence was cheerful and open with
clear views all about of the grounds and the life abounding
there, bringing a thin smile to her face as she spoke.

the light was particularly cruel to her emaciated, wasted face,
the wrinkles and flesh sagging about her, but she seemed as
usual, quite fearless in the face of death.

we sat for over an hour and revisited our original friendship,
our many laughs, her memories of her trips overseas, and
then, oddly, as we began the process of leaving, she had us
listen.

her voice, now feeble and lacking the intensity it once had,
still held us in place and she asked us to please fetch the box
under her bed.

B---- removed a very simple wooden box devoid of orna-
mentation from under the hospital bed. "open it," she ex-
claimed to us. it easily flipped open.

"those are all my fears," she told us, and we peered over one
another's shoulders for a better view. "I've kept them hidden
for so long, and now they are here for all to see."

her smile was radiant, and suddenly she seemed to be in her
early thirties again when we had first met her, vibrant and
alive, but as our eyes met over the box, we realized it was
empty.

she passed the next morning in her morning rest with no one
about, and that empty box of fears open and resting on her
dresser next to her jewelry box.

if we had only been able to find out from her what those
fears actually were, we might have been satisfied, but that
was now impossible.
the three of us who had been with her added the simple
wooden box to her also simple wooden coffin, and she was
buried peacefully while birds celebrated the spring day's
brilliance.

a riverbank

where we walk today besides the shrill stones
no one hears their call
but the leaning Tulip Poplar
the Weeping Willow

we cast out the common names randomly
like fishermen at the nets
hoping for a full return
a days reward

we wonder at what is here before us
the stones and the woods
laughing so hard and long
others stare at us

but like the children we are
our wonder multiples as we walk
kicking up the now-voiceless rocks
shuffling through the quiet leaves

believing as children do
tomorrow brings more
and more

My thanks to the editors and publishers of Truth Serum's
numerous anthologies, and I've just published in Truth
Serum's "Achievement"-themed anthology as part of their
Lifespan series the following:

all fall down

dreaming
she was dreaming
only that
she offered
her hand out-stretched
clutching at the thin coverlet
failing again and again to hold it
grasp it
asking me
is this a dream
did you bring this to me
fragments of red rose memory
her cracked red lips thin and dry now
did we make it
asking me with her eyes tightly closed
I love surprises you remember
no I allow
we didn't
it is still out there somewhere
and then she
in that remarkable burst of clarity
recited Humpty Dumpty
and we all fall down

like today

intermittent sunshine
cloud breaks
mare's tails
wisps snapped off

I ran through the bed sheets
pinned to the cotton clothes line
wooden pegs
sun fresh cloth whipped my face

like today when I heard sheets popping
someone on St. Claude drying sheets
clothes vibrant color flagging
summon me home

summon me away from today
summon smells so fresh and so distant
I stand immobile immutable
I hear a voice I know from then
calling me inside
calling me away from today
but all I wish
is to stand and smell the past

I hear bird calls

I hear bird calls behind the hanging fog
thinking how lovely the sound
how lucky I am
in these hard times to hear them
somewhere in a dense evergreen hedge

I wonder if you hear them too
or if you ignore them as most do
forgetting that one day
you'll hear nothing ever again
as you pass to star dust

this is the way of us rushing about
always looking but not seeing
listening but not hearing
talking about absolutely nothing
ignoring the music of our universe

a feral cat stands by the hedge
pebble-hard eyes unblinking
its tail switches its displeasure
but I cannot turn away
if it were a bird it would disappear
identical in color as the fog

it is entangled in its hunger
and I am entangled in it
in it all

the broken house at the end of the busted road

the broken house at the end of the busted road
was an immigrant families house
Latvians
left at the old train station post WWII
employed by a small cotton planter
until the family left for Chicago
fifteen years later

before then it had been another's house
three rooms and an out house behind
slowly sliding into the dust
the Delta winds blow
across Arkansas and the River
but the old woman died
there in that house

and she was buried in the old Methodist cemetery
her name erased by that same wind and dust

then the house became part of the cotton planters
scant holdings and was expanded
five rooms and indoor toilet
LP gas squatting
toad-like outside the windows
where those Latvians
raised three kids
then moved on

the last time I saw the house and this has been
some time ago now as the years fly
no one had lived there
maybe a squatter or two
soon chased off by
the planter and his growing sons

one Halloween the house caught fire magically
some say it was intentionally set
by those sons as a prank
but it wouldn't burn
remained scorched in its back rooms
and sadly
now
is sliding to its left off the
concrete and brick pilings

and the road is full of buckthorn and privet
johnson grass tall as the roof of
my car

Iggy's On The Corner

Touro and North Rampart / hanging / pull out a
chair / smokers seats / you got sixty cents / music
eddying / smoke eddying / talk eddying about the
day / modern times I hear / toothless guy whistles
while he talks / sax cuts right through the haze /
humid / wisteria blooming / why argue / Sammy
likes it / getting loud outside /

Sshhhhh / neighbors complaining / sax solo / heads
bopping / our sound / our
town / in the Marigny / wachu gonna do / it goes
along / it goes on / picks up / settles
down / drifts along / then bops out again / Touro
and North Rampart / Bobby come
out / stretches / looks around / whachall doin /
chairs scrape / Bobby can be trouble /
gettin me a gin and tonic / listening to the saxophone
/ curling around me like a cat /
wants to be scratched / arches its back / Touro and
North Rampart / the clock stuck on

Awarded publication in the Summer, 2021, French
Quarter Journal poetry contest.
July, 2021.

passing this way again

while I pass through here today
listening to the faint rumble of before-dawn thunder
and voices from a bus stop shelter
like stars mumbling among themselves

all things revealed slowly to me
passing this way again amidst the accumulated trash
swept into my bordering gutter
tiny rivers cascading to their sea

there I find modern failure heaped into a cardboard temple
only an arm waving majestically
only a voice within that structure
reminding me of our duty

but it's all-seeing eye reveals me as I pass
calls out to me as reminder
as accused
as repeat offender

and I am the only one who hears
as I hurry to my warm rooms

Some Day the River Come'n

walking on Esplanade a fine blue Saturday morning
surveying tree damage, leaf clutter, torn signs
everywhere the stench of rotting garbage,
produce, refrigerator debris, wet miscellaneous

I stopped to watch a line of power company trucks creep by

overheard two passing people talking
storms and hurricanes and such

wasn't much to this'un
was out towds Metairie
next'un could be a worse'un
oh you wadn't alive when theys bad
I wud heah fo 'trina
that right! that wuz one Bad Bitch
had nine feet a water in Treme
levee broek on da lake
ain't gonna happen again
but
some day the river come'n
that'd be the las one

so it goes here, always the River
waiting like some mythic monster
just over there beyond the Riverwalk
where you can buy beignets and the trolley turns around

I walk on

Another Man Done Gone

star dust returned in finer quality that it was loaned
with it went accumulated fears, hopes, dreams, loves,
passions, and few if any base thoughts
he was never judgmental of me
another man done gone from me
I've watched the ranks depleted often as if by magic
here one moment, then gone
I will miss this one's infinite patience and practicality
I will miss his sensibility and mindfulness
his calm, his humanity
we are less now, having lost this piece of us
it was enough that he was here 73 years
it will have to do
another man done gone

the artist who was a butterfly

eerily quiet Sunday morning on Royal at Orleans
behind St Louis Cathedral
one artist sprawls across the torn sidewalk
drawing butterfly wings on cheap paper
his labors piled by his side
as he stretches his arms over his head in relief
he appears to be a resting butterfly
wings folded above the still form
I ask about his work
he refuses any intrusion
tightly draws his legs toward his chest
pulls his papers into him
it has begun to mist
the early call to prayer sounds from the bell tower
hauntingly hollow from where I stand
I turn and walk quickly away
one backward glance
hoping to catch his metamorphosis
but he has already flown
translucent wings carrying him far above me
over the tiled rooftops
leaving nothing behind
but the memory

the plans we unmade

like the bed we unmade
or the coin we didn't toss
the step not taken
the card we didn't turn over

how do we face the next
and the next
in this life
we unplanned for

so
hard question times
when we reach the edge of the map
why won't we step over
the clock winds down
ignore it
unwind it

risks are to be confronted
challenge confronted
in that is life
peering at us
eye to eye
on even terms
met and met

Thanks to the editors of "flea-bitten dog" for including the
following poem, "the saints go marching in,"in its on-line
literary publication.

The saints go marching in

this Sunday morning as it is and has been each and every
Sunday morning
the saints go marching in
that same squat clapboard church
sitting somnolently other days under an ancient sycamore

its two front windows
framing a plain white-washed door
seem to watch me pass by
watch all pass by but Sunday
placidly waiting the saints arrival

and this Sunday morning
as surely as sunrise and moonset
the minister's new Cadillac pulls up in front
and within moments the church is alive again
awaiting the saints

the Word is spoken and spread among the saints
their voices raise in praise
blessing all within and those passing
wooden floors creak and groan
accompanied by the scuffling of pews

by mid-afternoon the service has been over
lunch shared and eaten
solid women and the scant few men slow to leave
stand in the dusty yard
saints reluctant to march home

our day is blessed
labors relieved until Monday morning
when the fields fill with equipment
women hum in their starched uniforms
and the slow gleaning of souls shines on

NOLA Haiku

Galleries bright lights,
Rue Royal dressed for Christmas
Rain-washed streets glisten

William Butler:

Butler has been writing since the mid 1960's with
his work appearing in various regional
and national literary publications. He has published
three books; two collections of poems
and one of short stories.

ISBN: 978-969-41-9291-8

www.ingramcontent.com/pod-product-compliance
Lightning Source LLC
Chambersburg PA
CBHW070811170726
48000CB00017B/360